# Ganvié Colouring Book

It is well documented that, for many people (adults and children alike), colouring is a therapeutic, stress-relieving pastime.

What could be better, then, than colouring in images of the vibrant floating village of Ganvié in Benin, West Africa?  Known as the 'Venice of Africa', Ganvié, with its stilt houses and brightly painted buildings, makes a great subject for a colouring book.

Unlike most other colouring books which are usually filled with whimsical and cartoon images, mine are full of real pictures.

In this case, the colouring pages were created from photographs I took during a Dragoman tour of West Africa.  We spent a glorious couple of days in Ganvié, getting to know the people and learning about their way of life.  Life happens on the water.  Everyone goes everywhere by boat – to school, to work, to the shops.  Market stalls are in boats.  We were lucky enough to be in Ganvié on a Sunday when the whole village turns out in their best clothes to go to church and to visit family.  The scene viewed from the restaurant upstairs in our floating hotel was a riot of colour, music and laughter.

Grab your favourite pens or pencils and let your imagination and creativity run riot.  I use high quality fine-tip felt pens for the details, and coloured pencils for the larger areas, but the choice is yours.  Some people like to put a water colour wash across the whole picture before they begin.  It's your creation.  It's up to you!

Cut out your finished work and display it somewhere as in inspiration to travel further for longer, or as a reminder of places you've already been to.

**Keep in touch with me at Happy Days Travel Blog or on social media:**

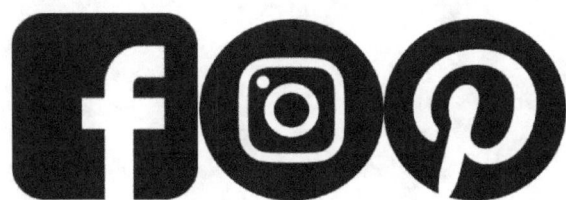 

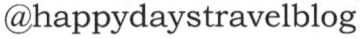

@happydaystravelblog          @happydayswriter

**Show me your creations, follow my travels and tell me about yours!**

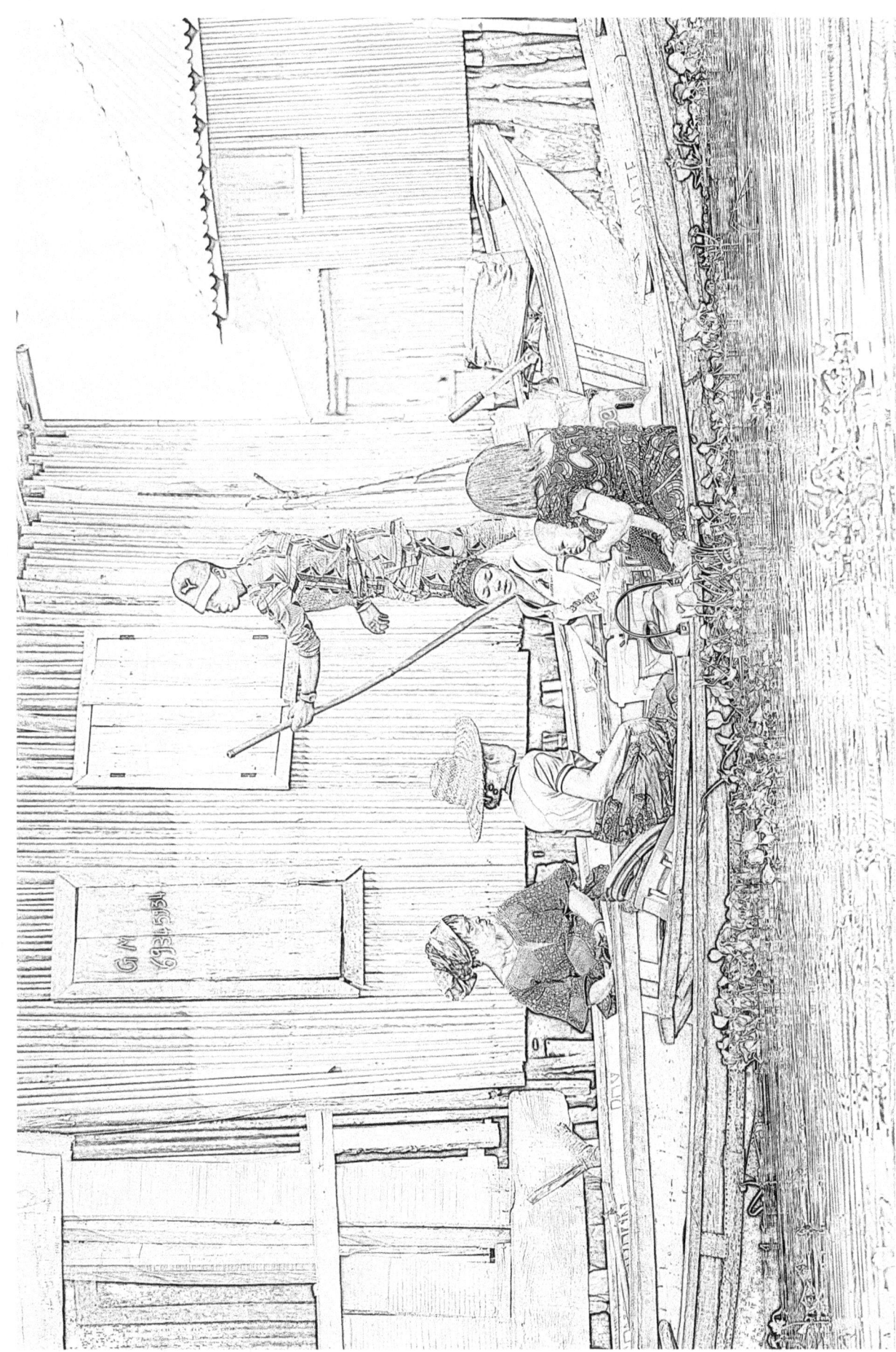

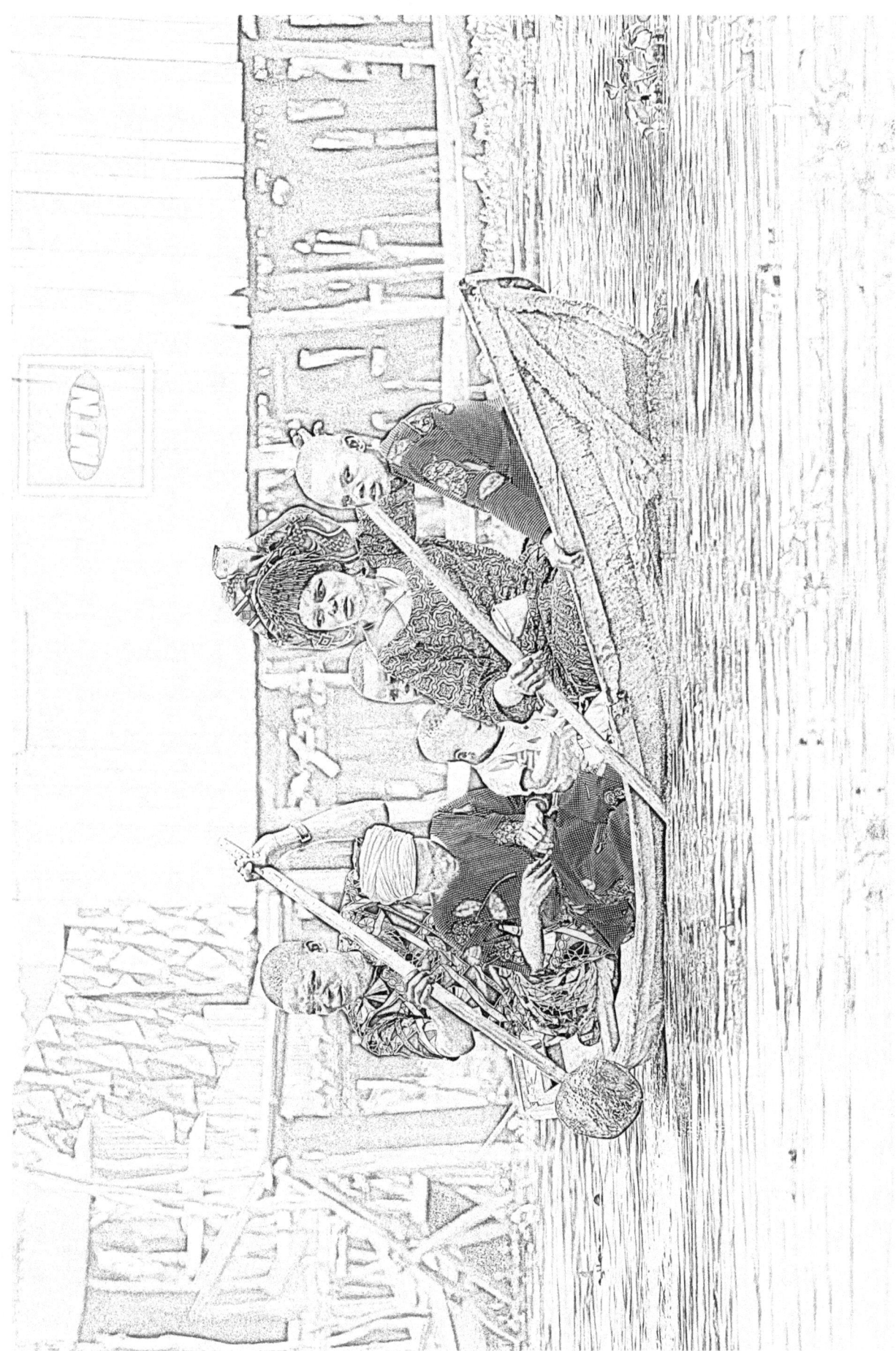

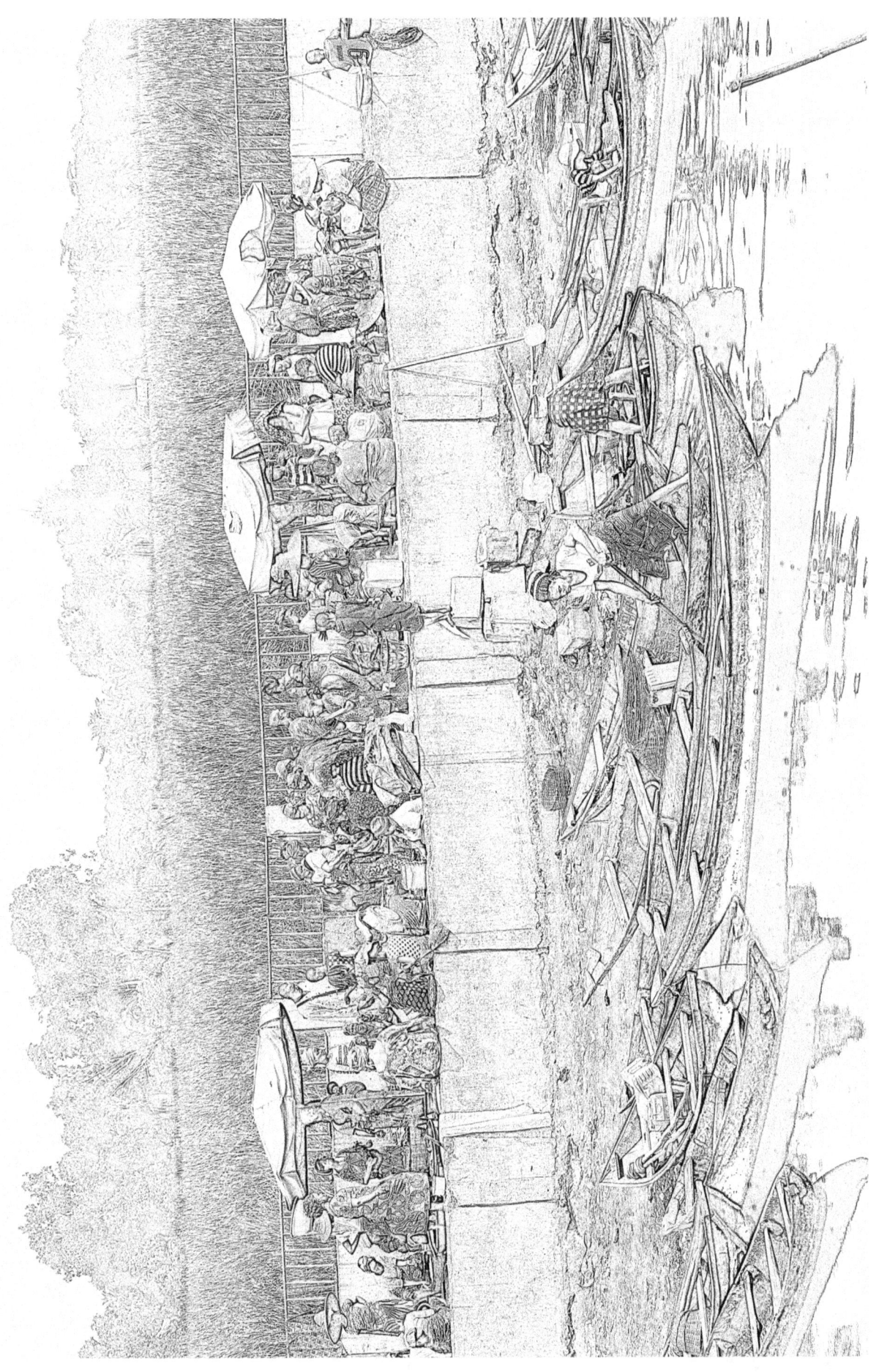

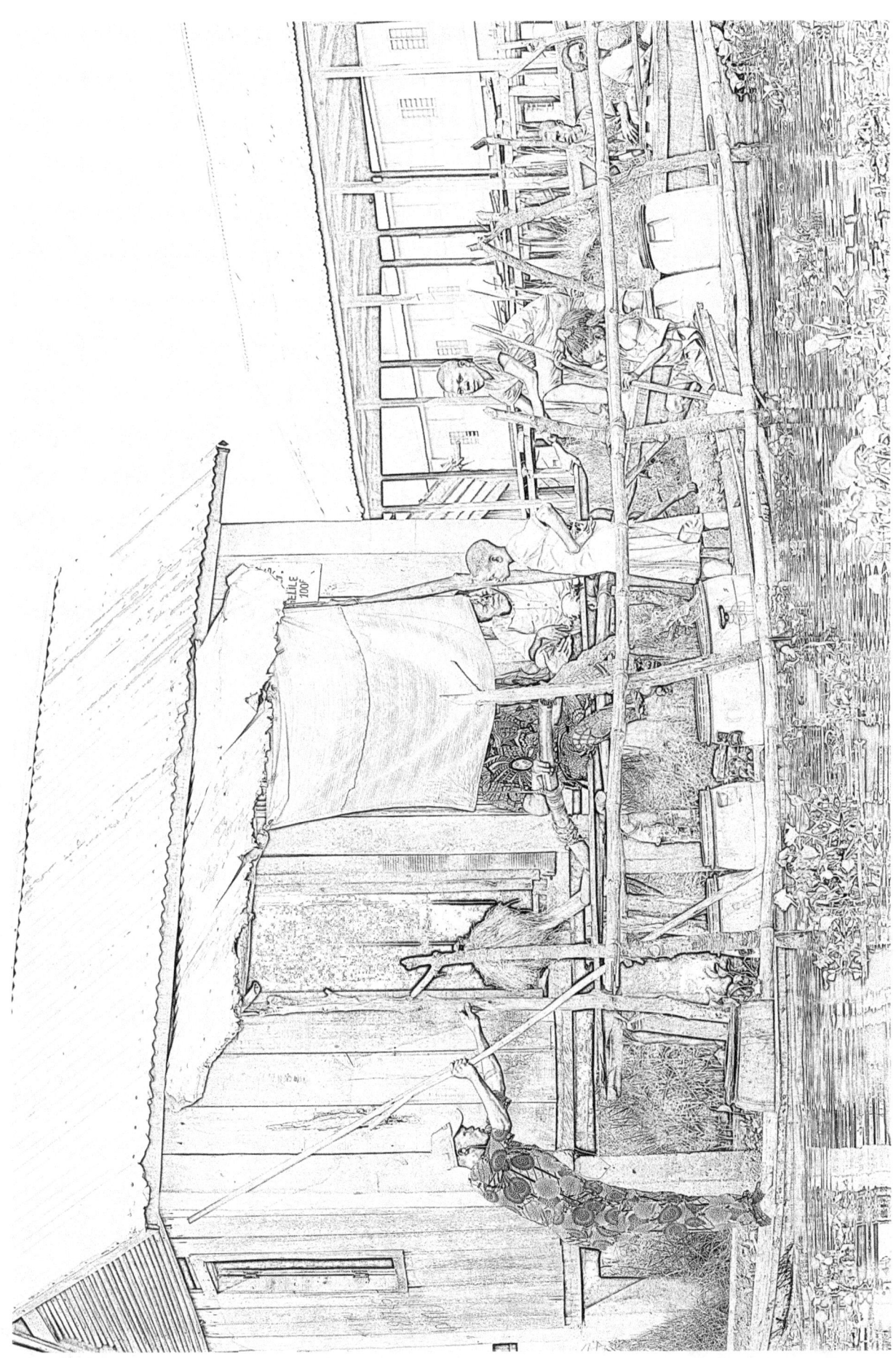

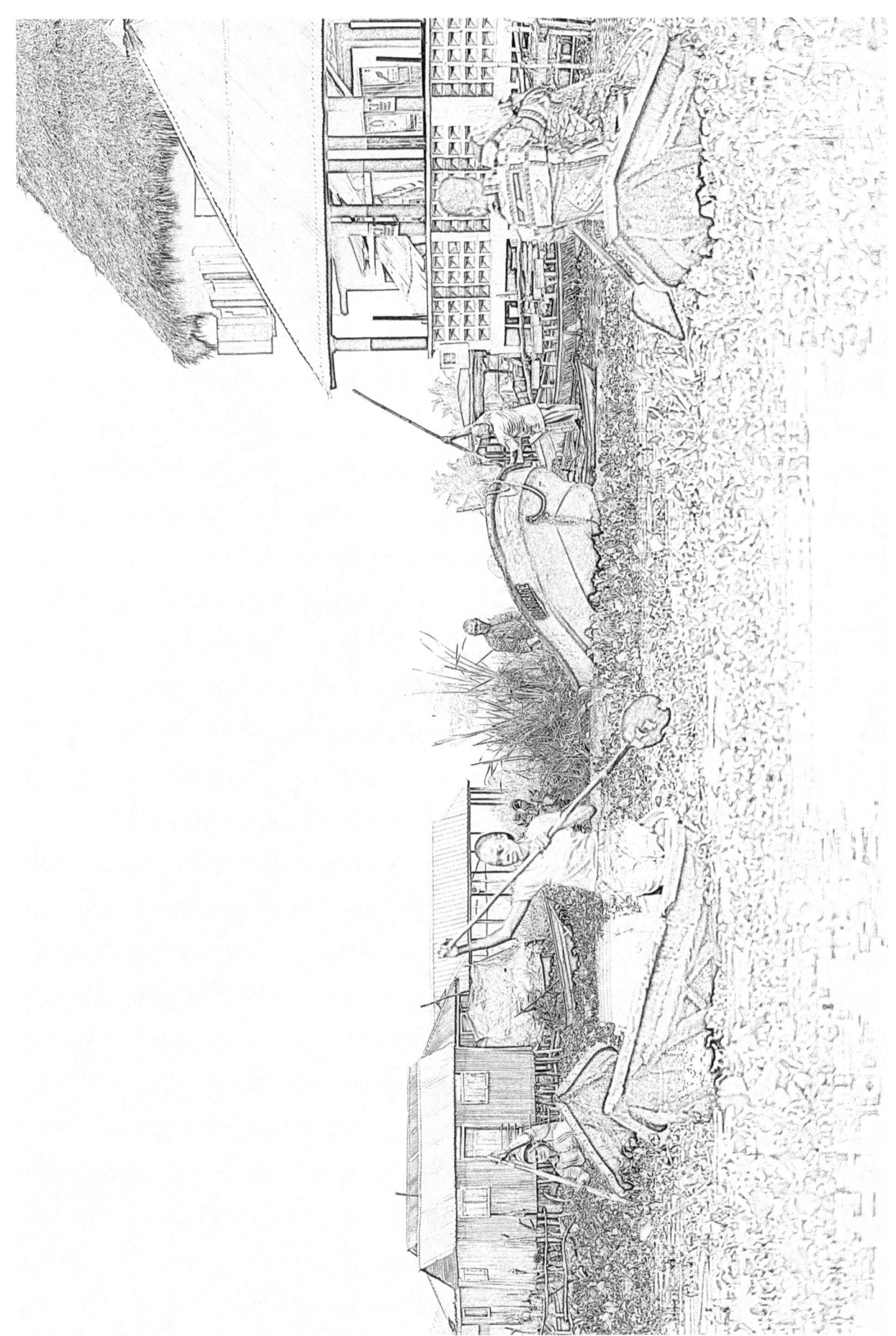

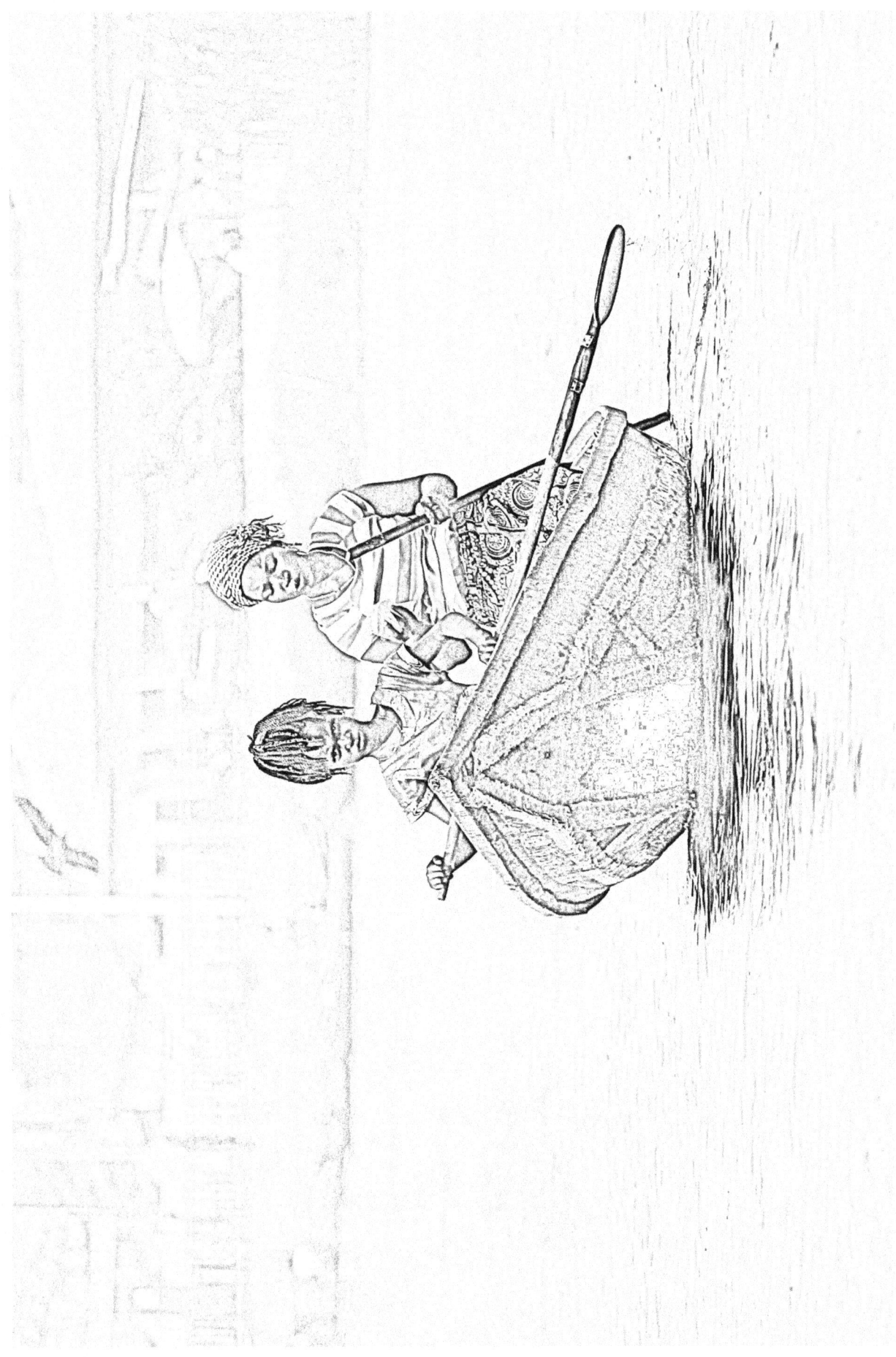

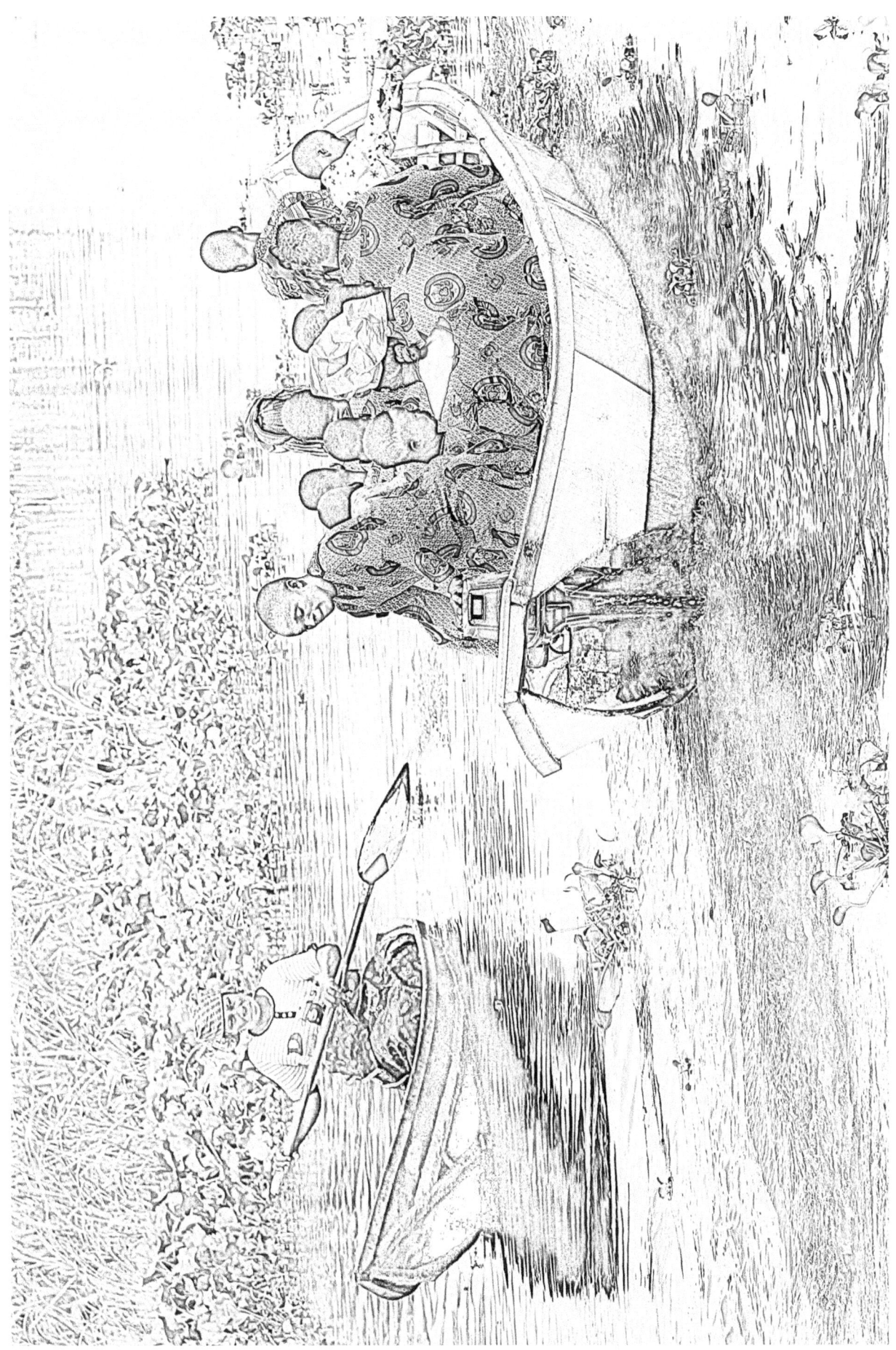

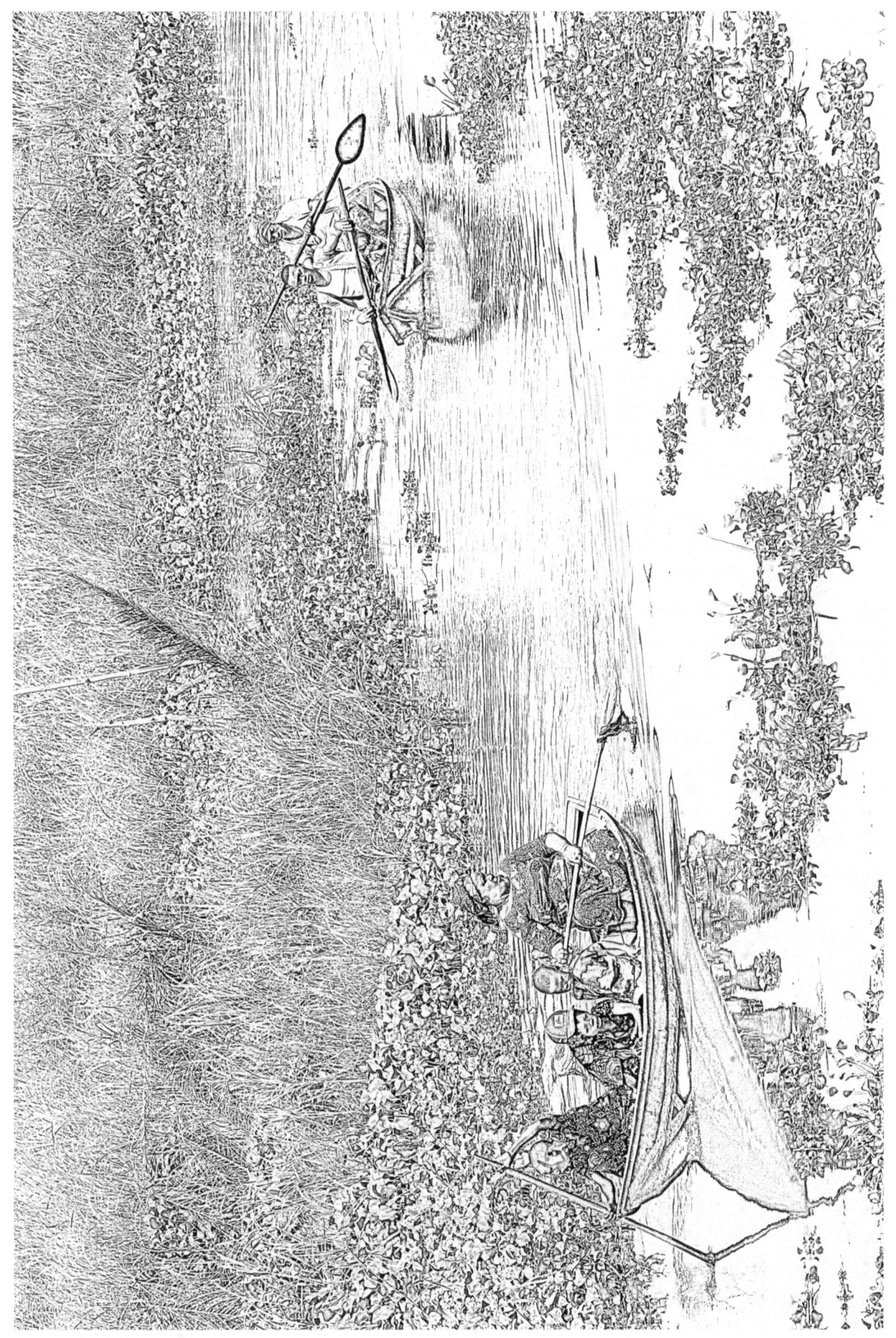

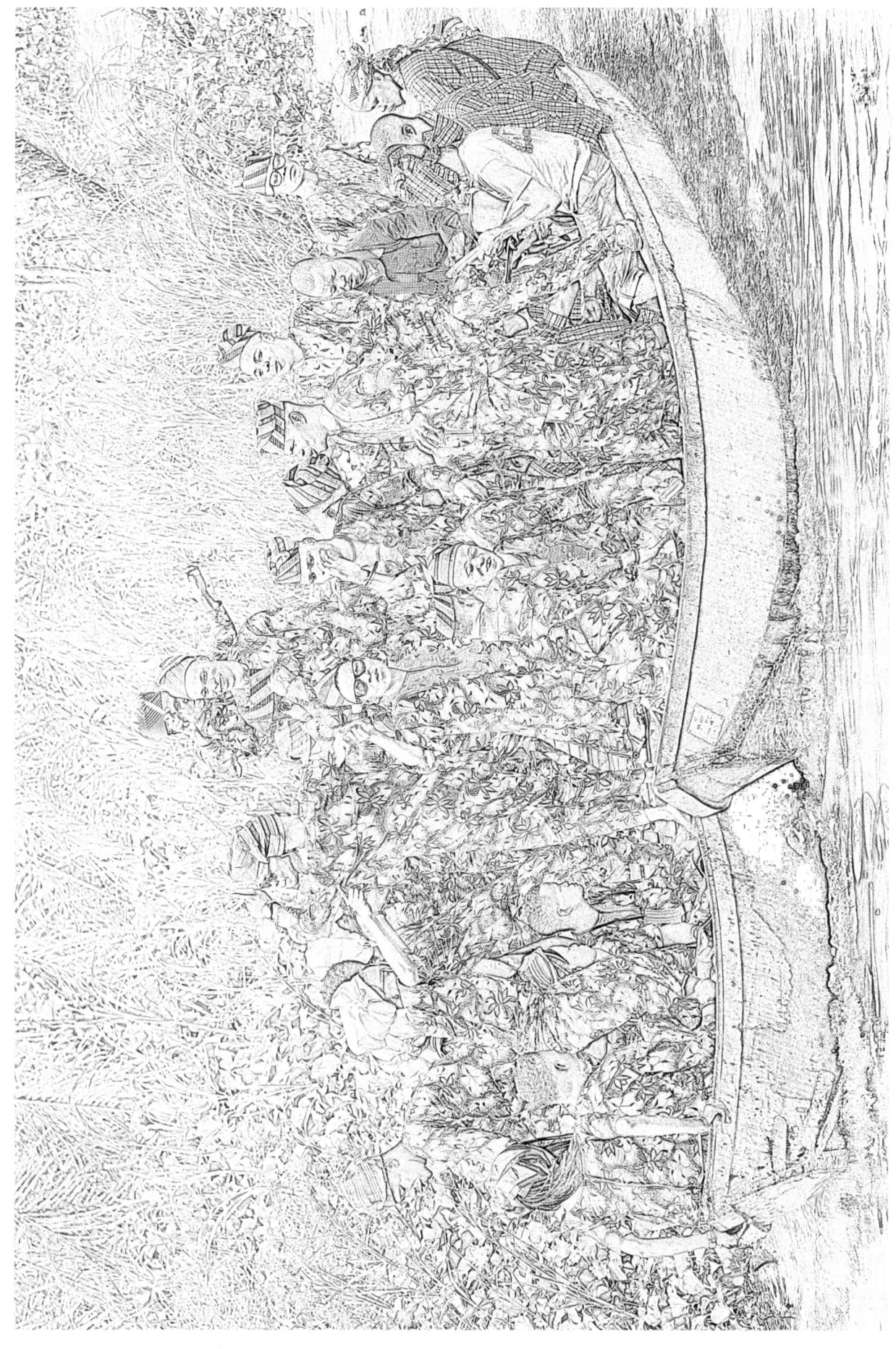

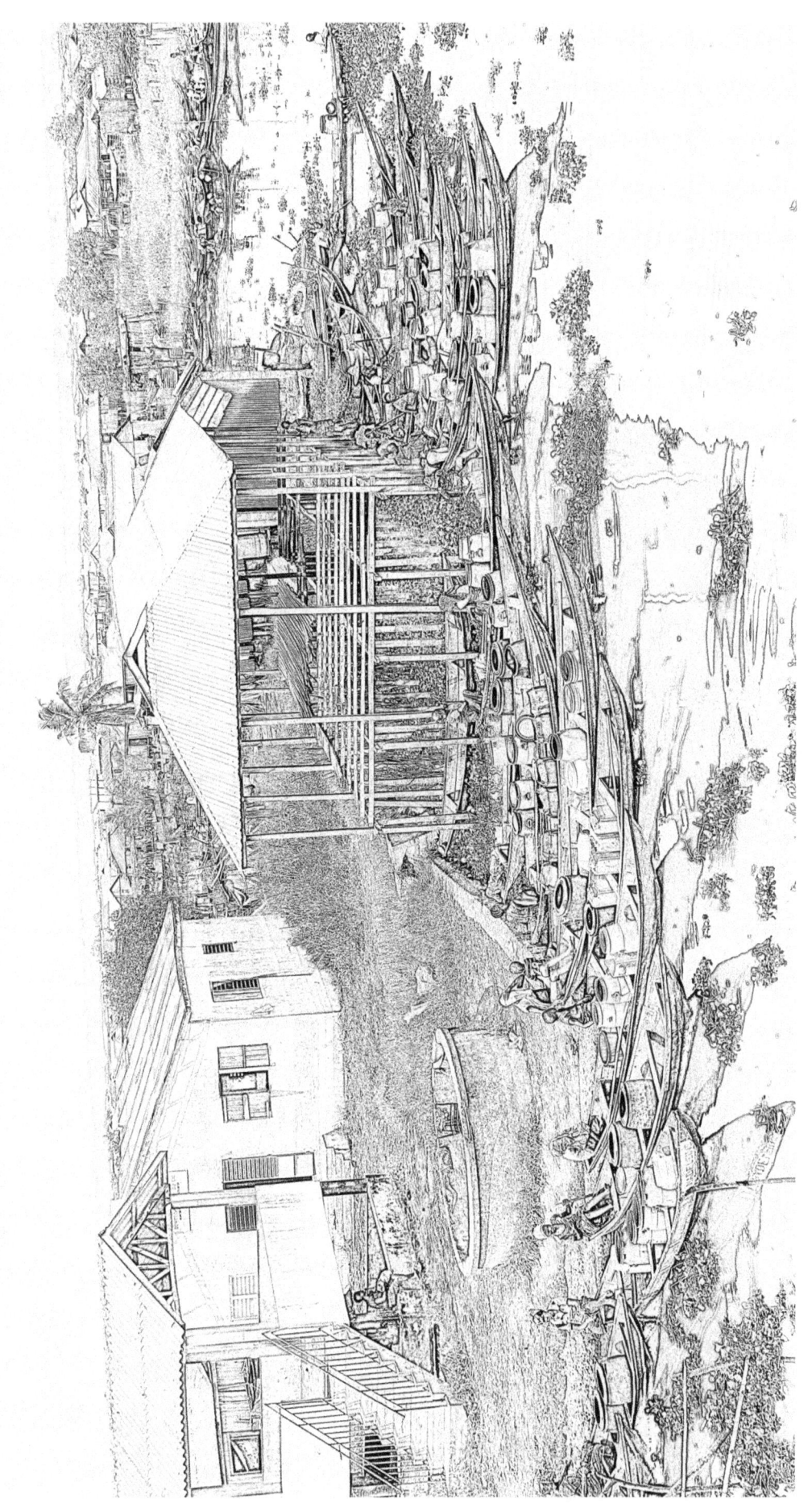

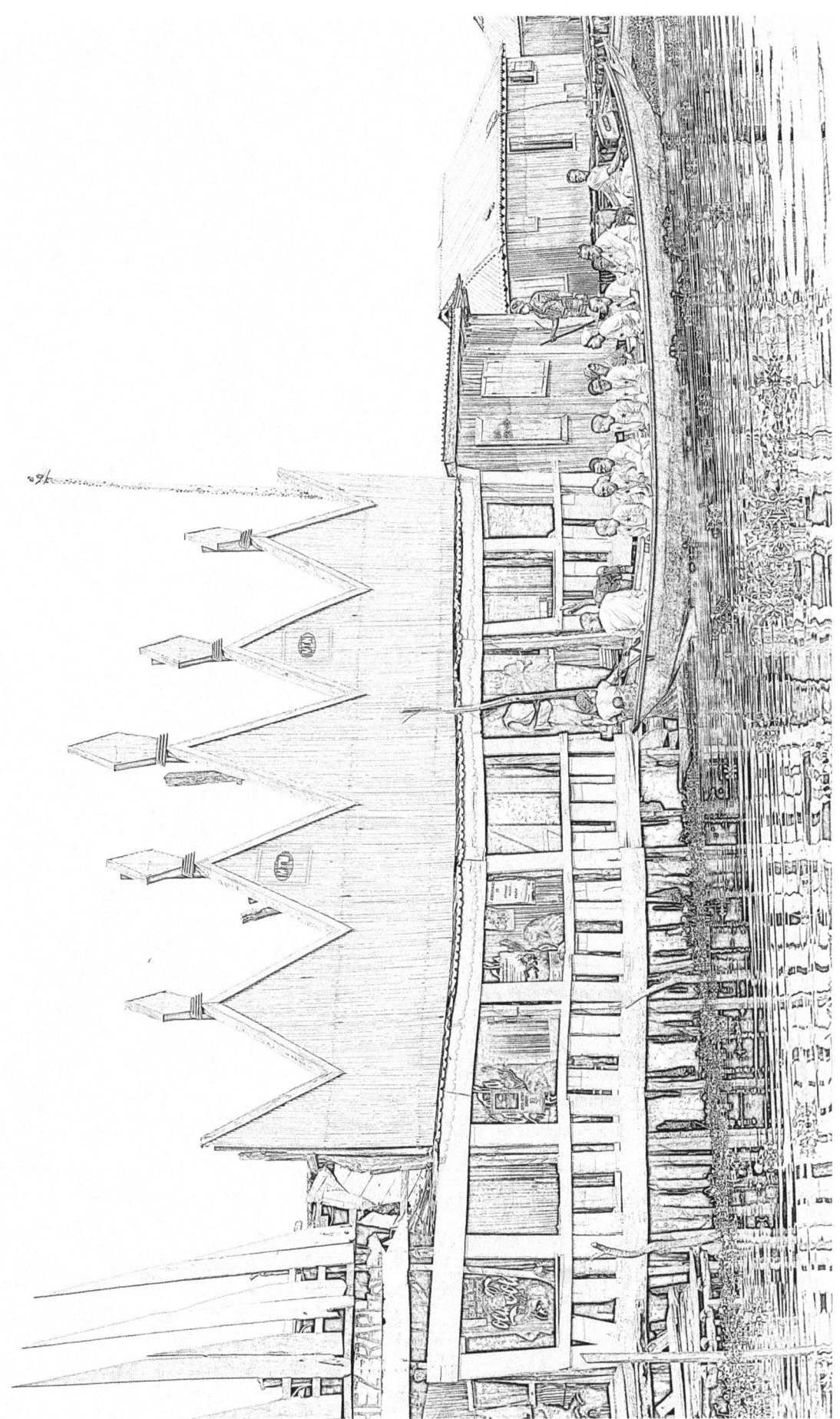

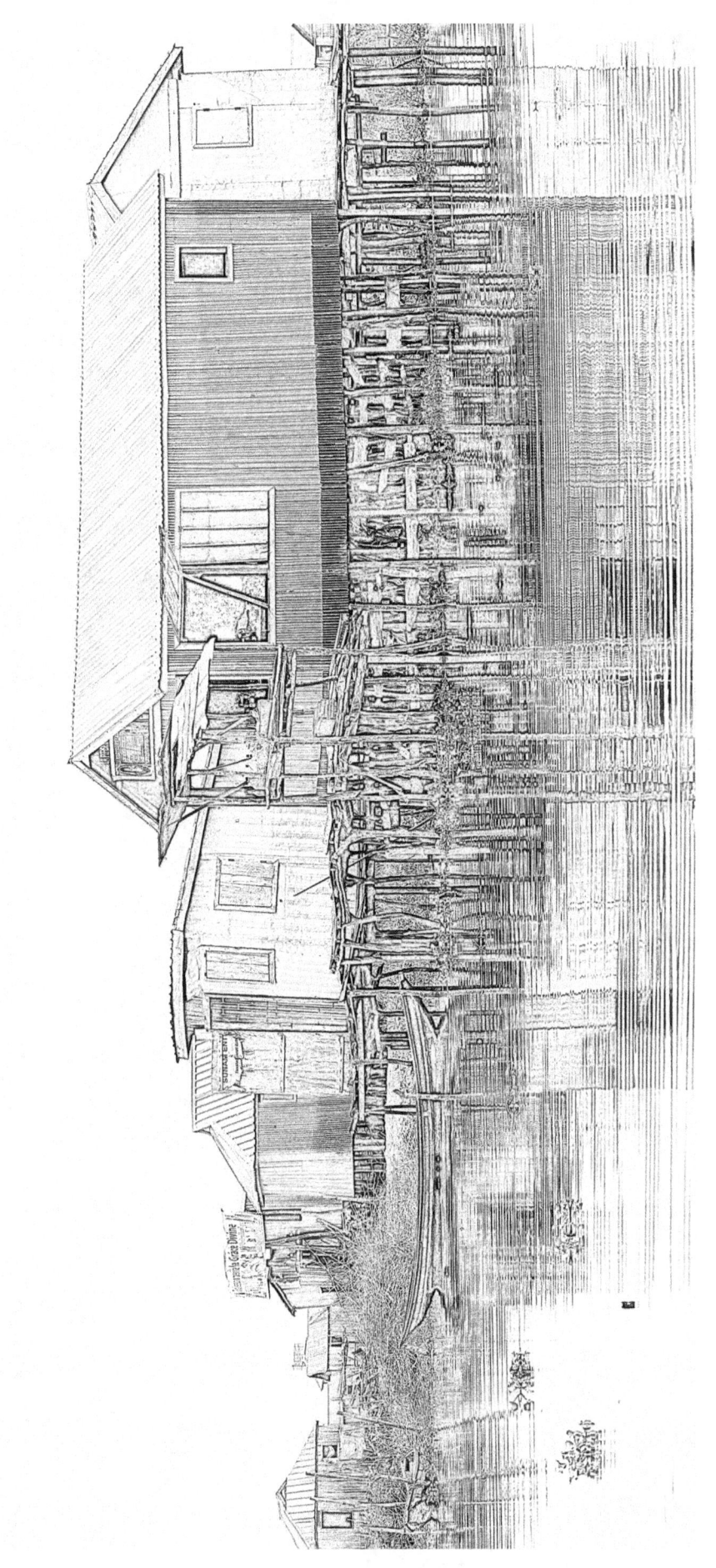

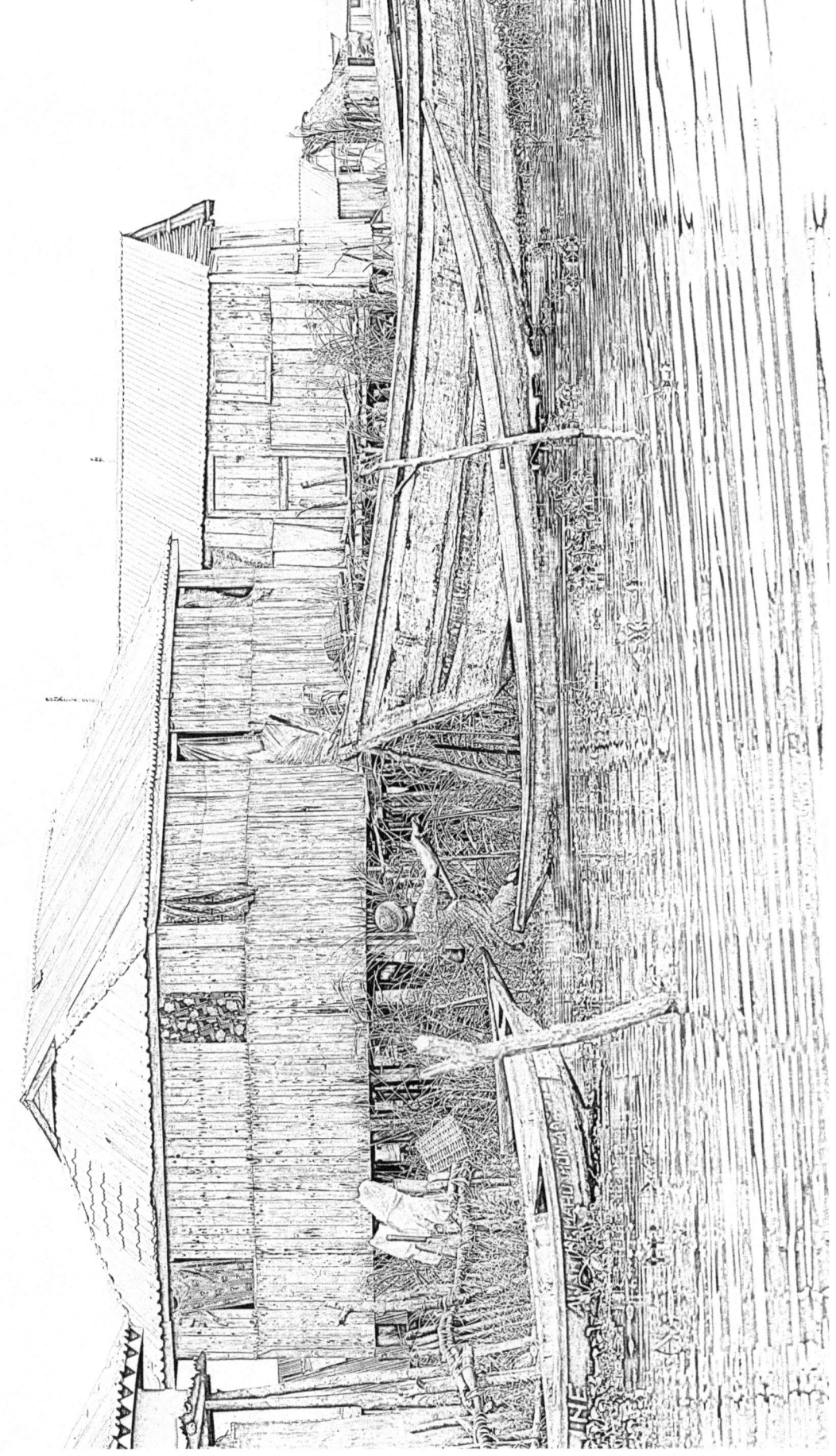

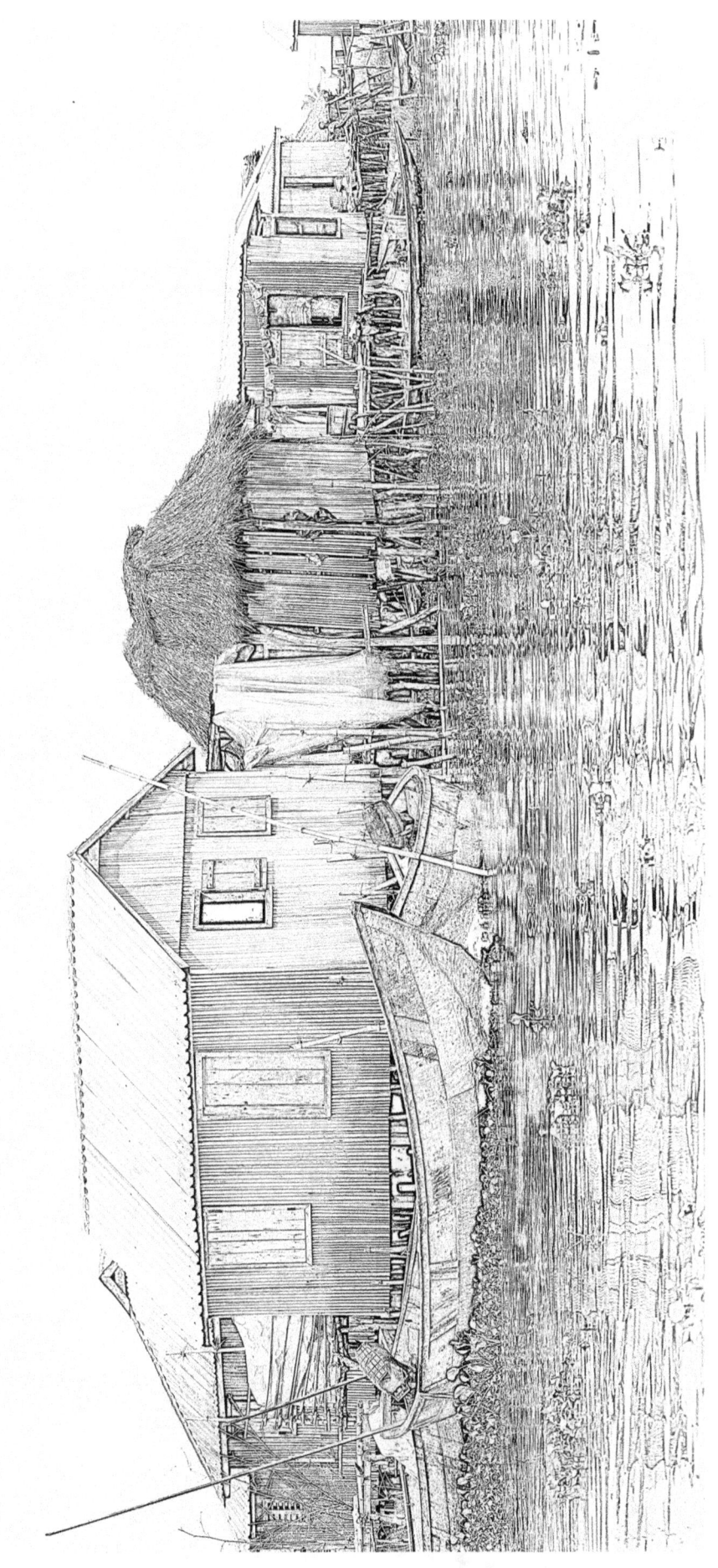

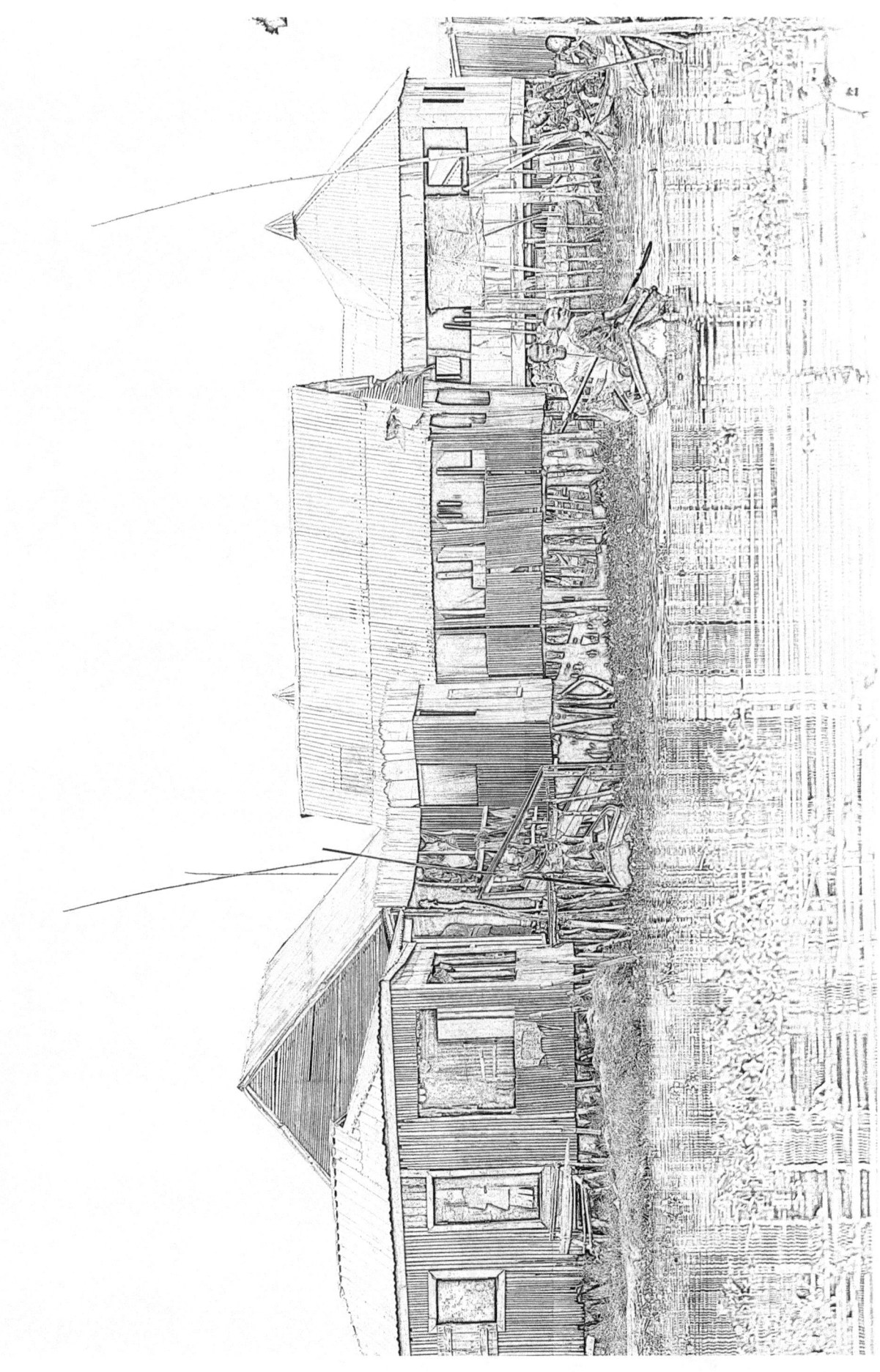

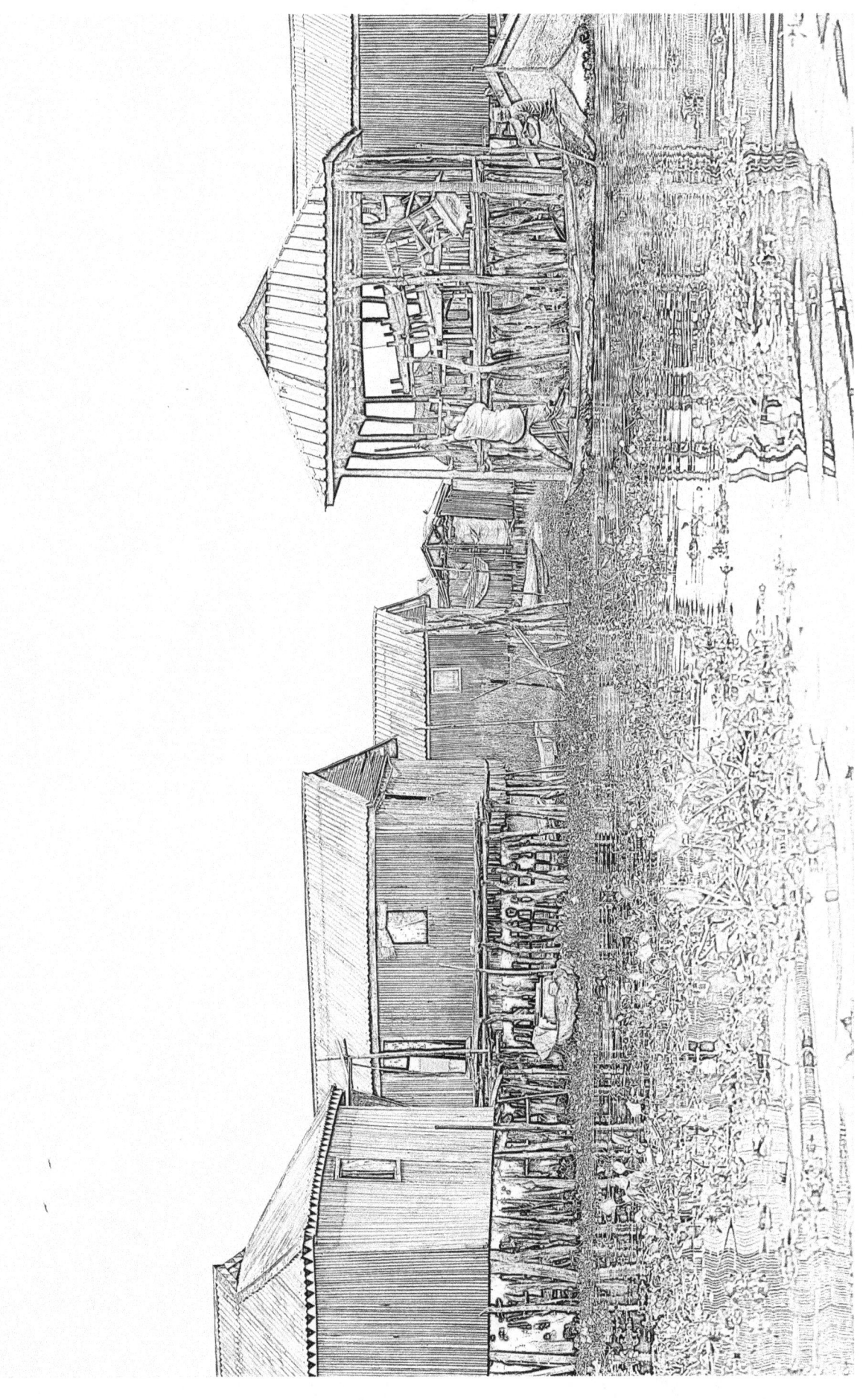

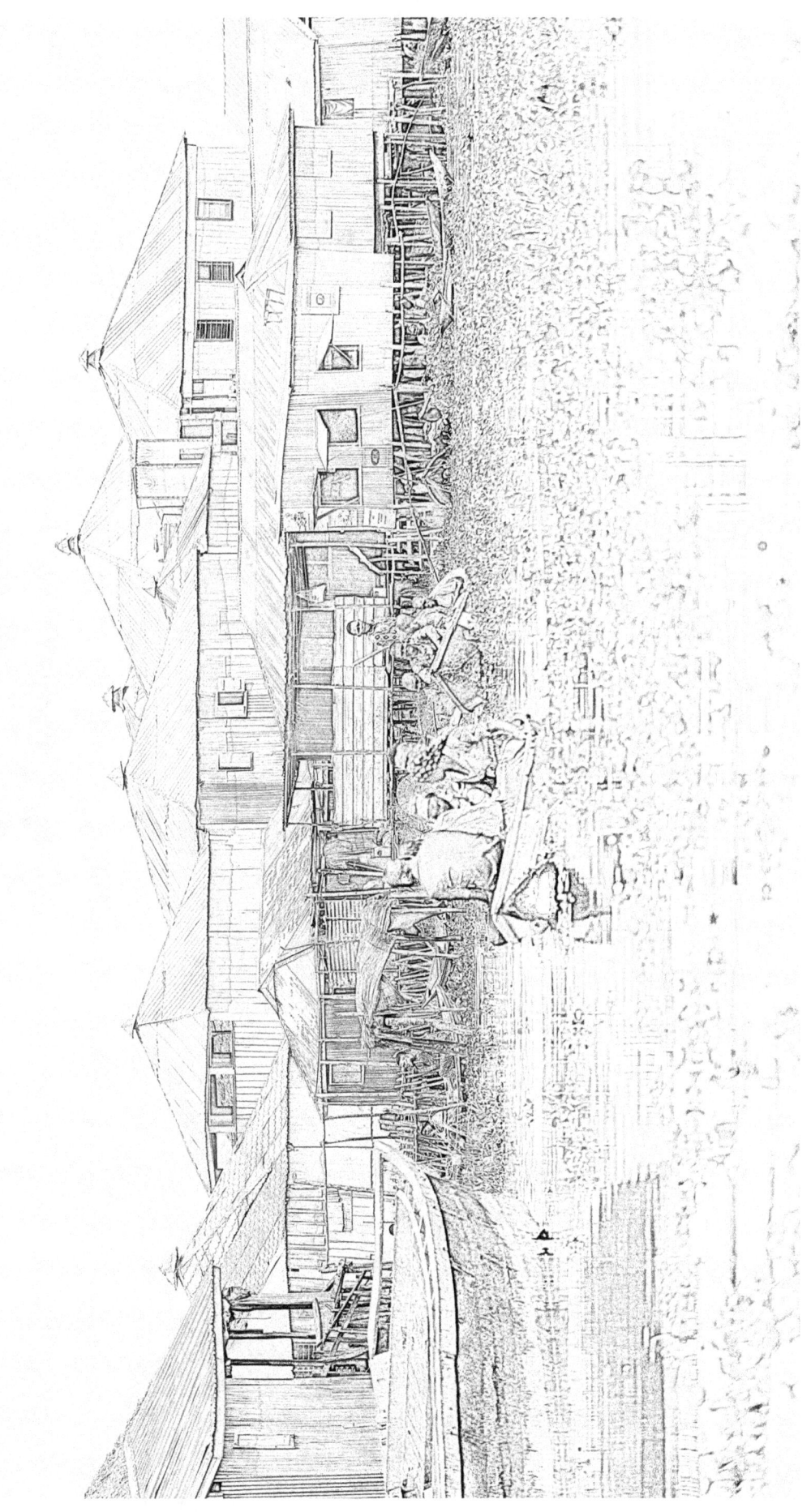

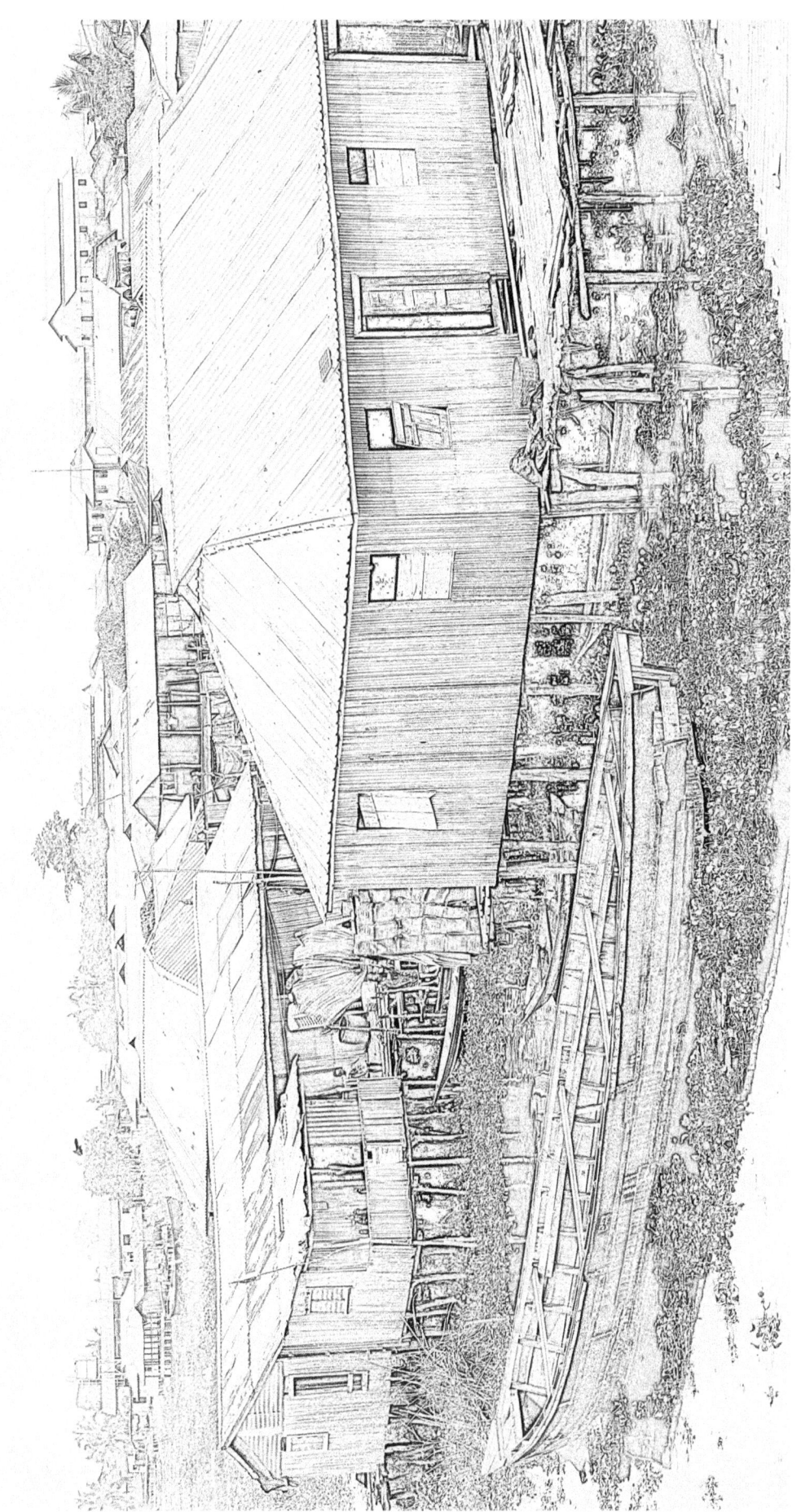

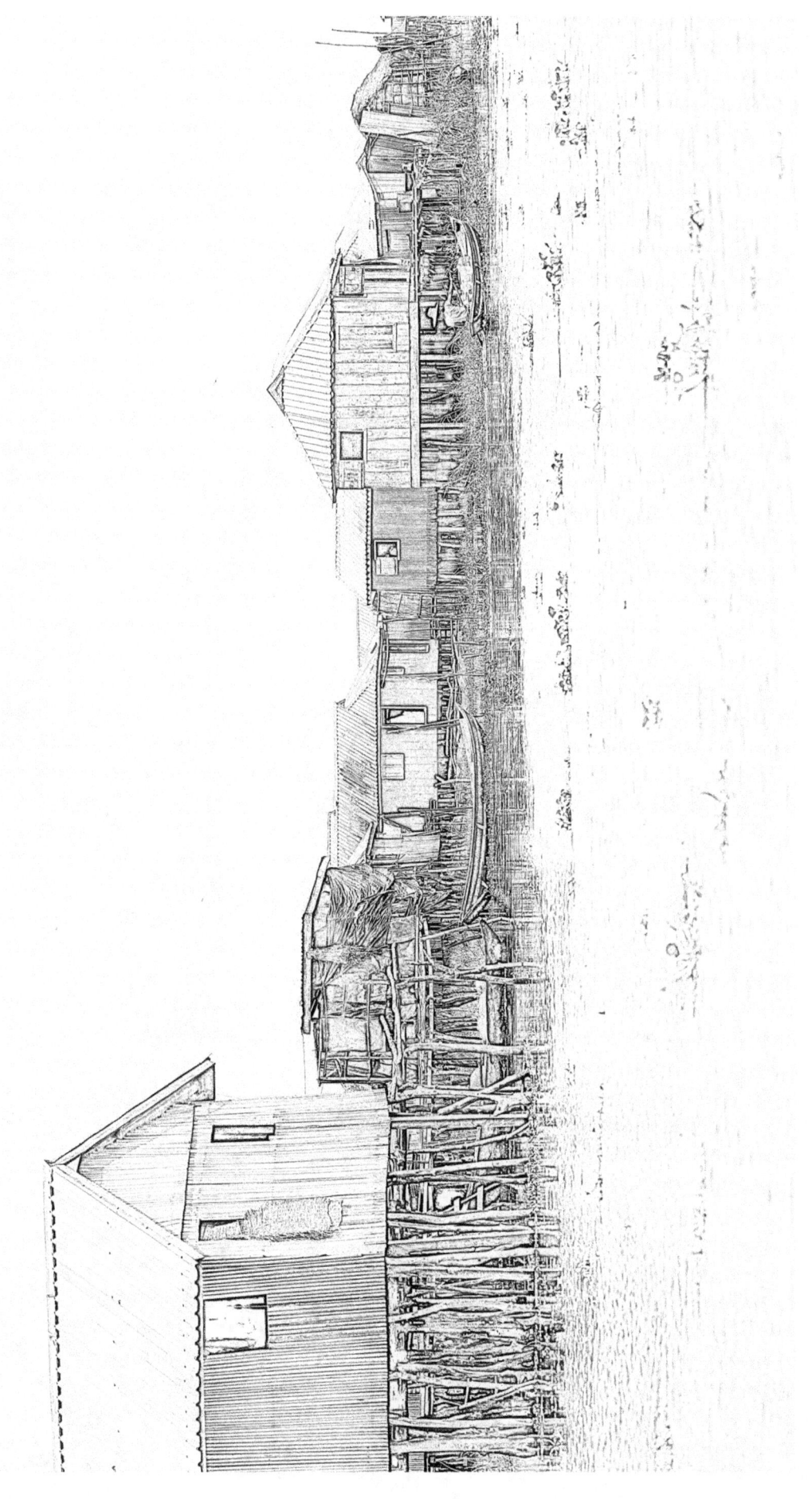

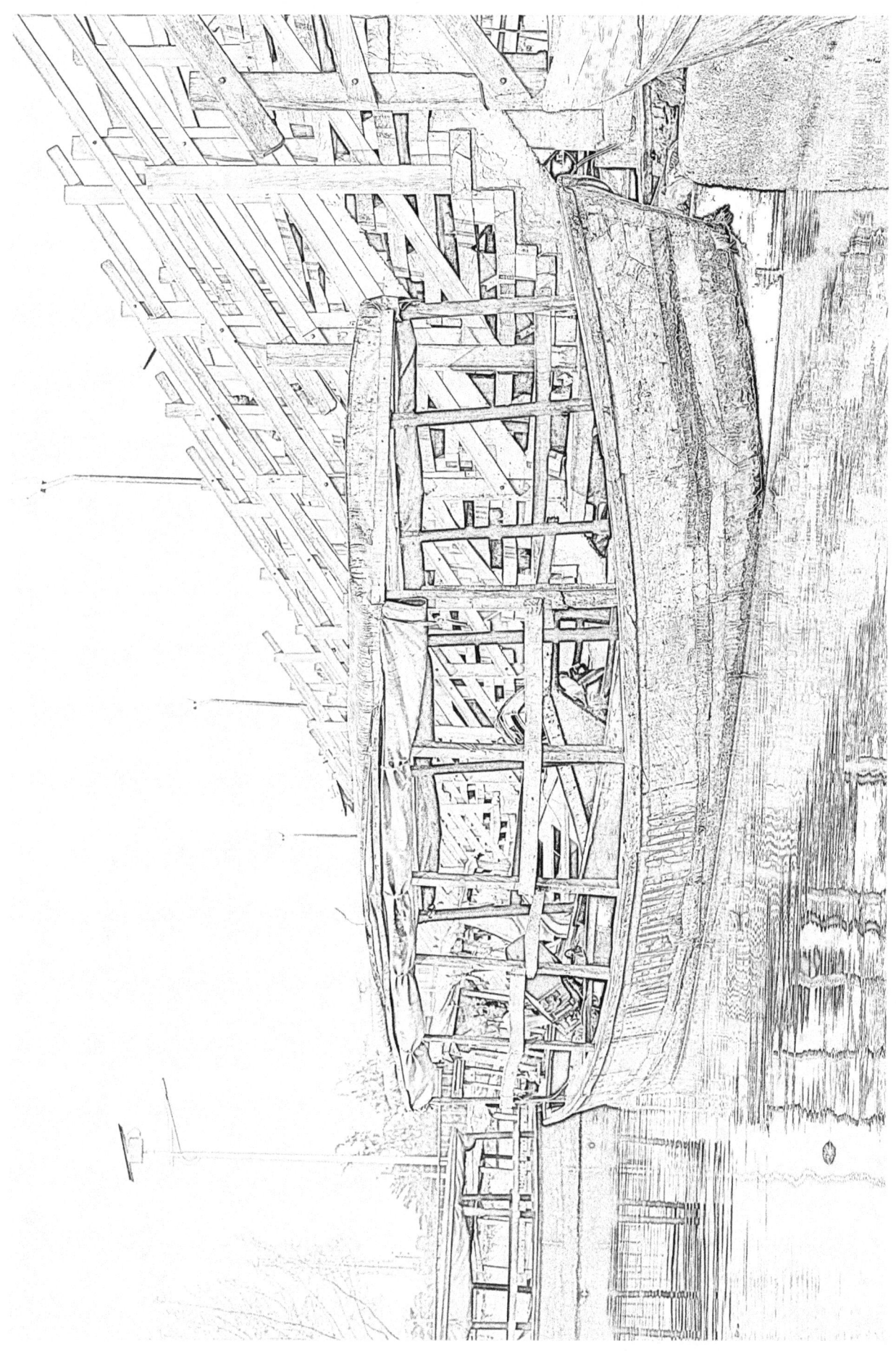

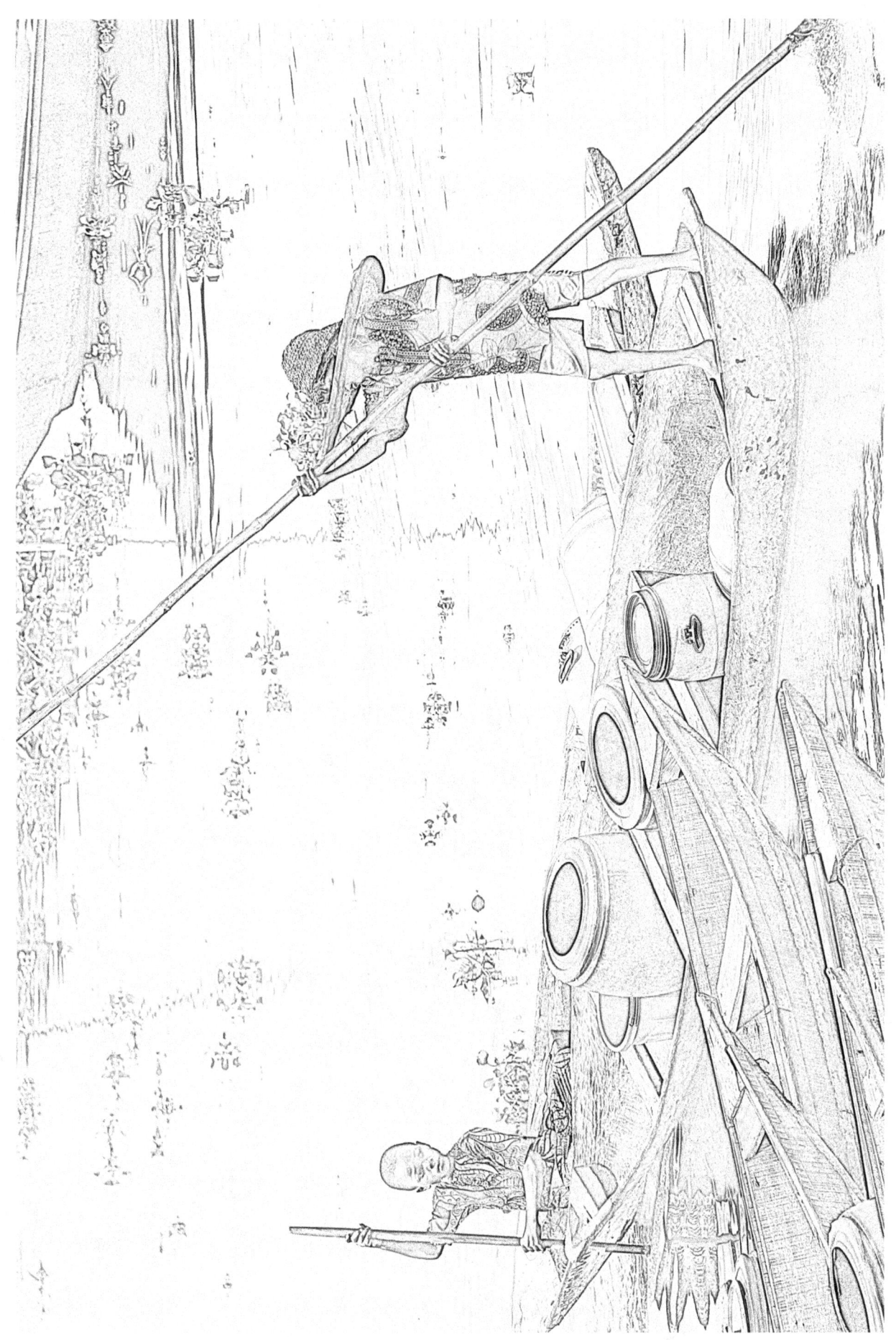

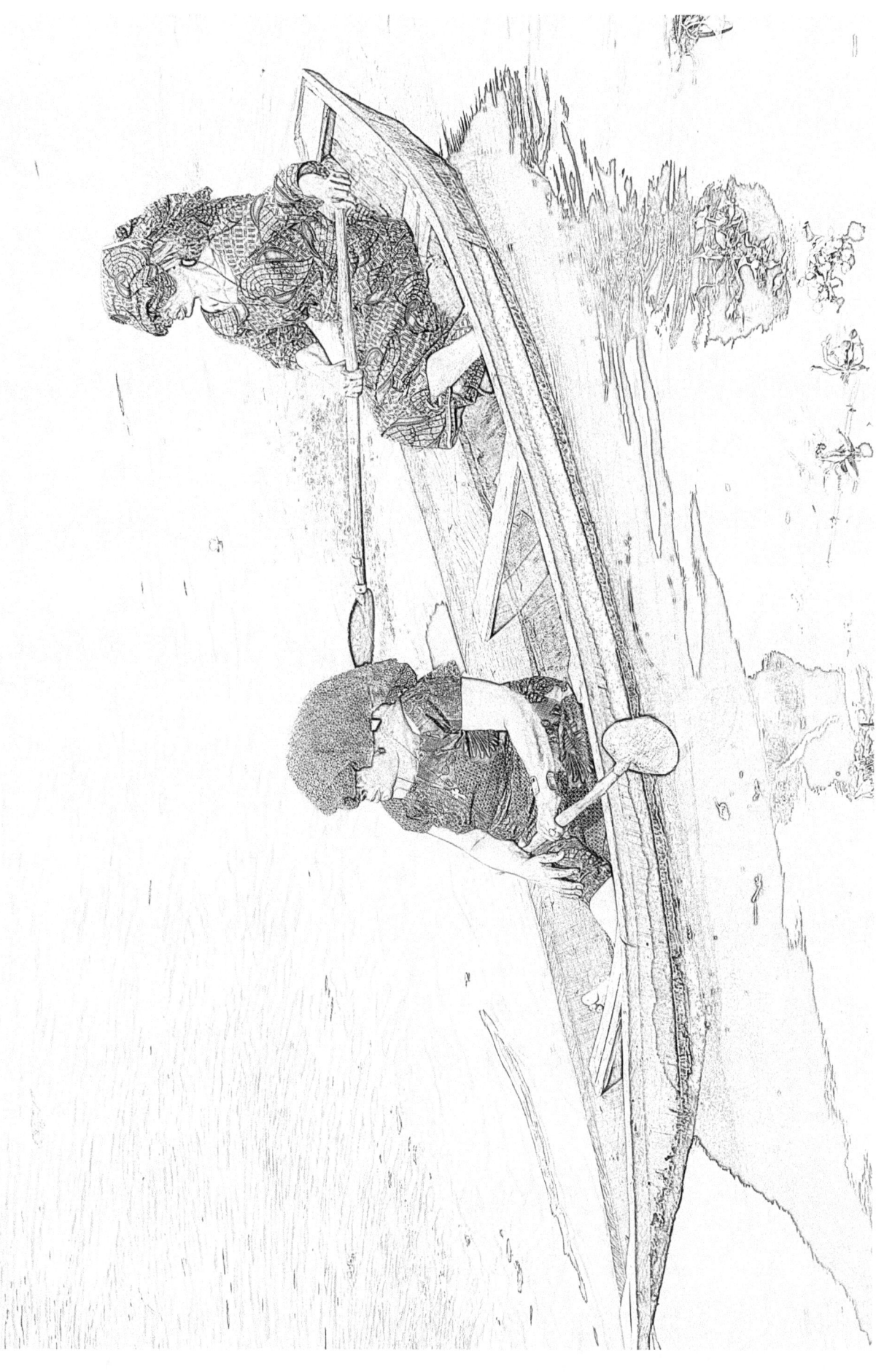

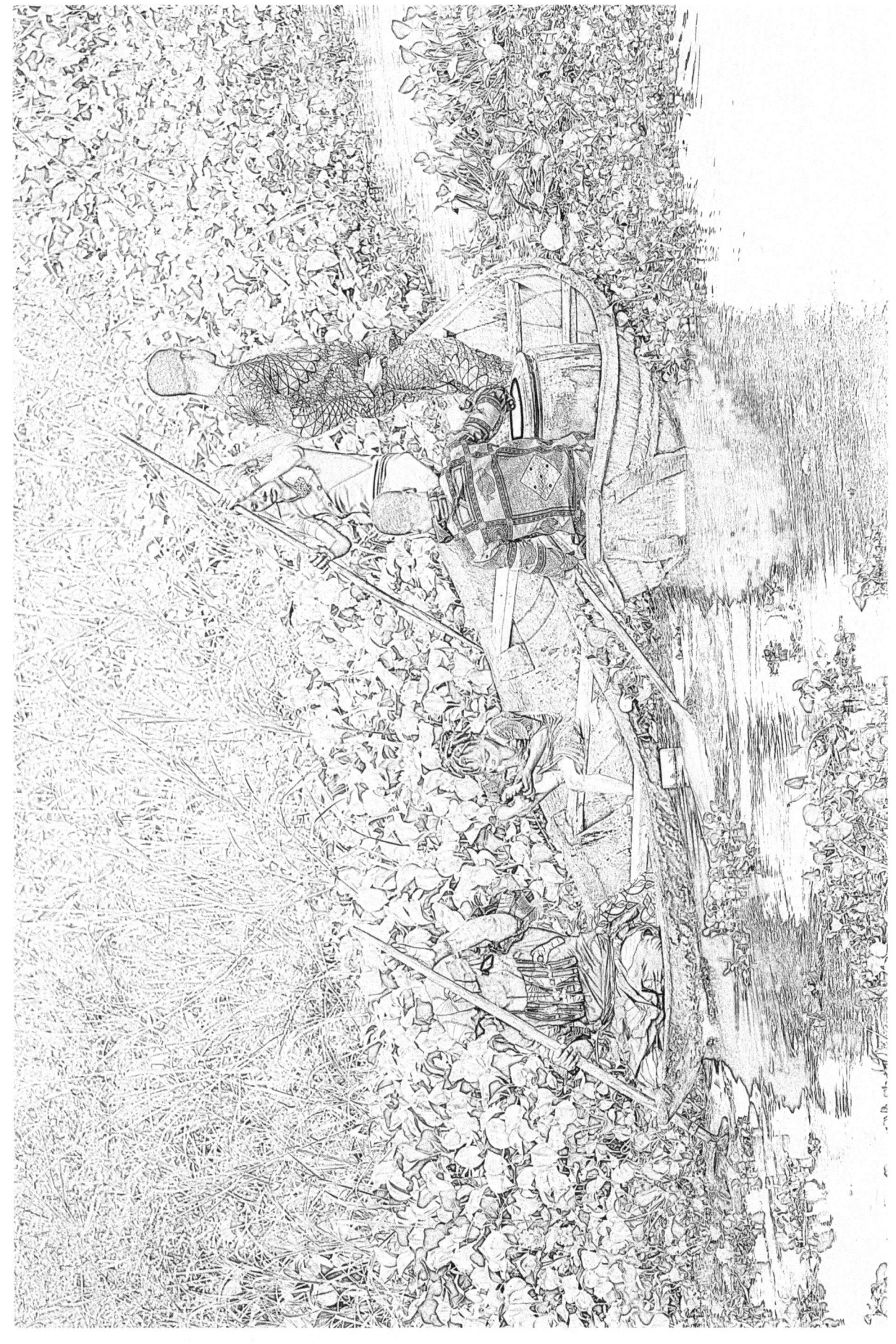

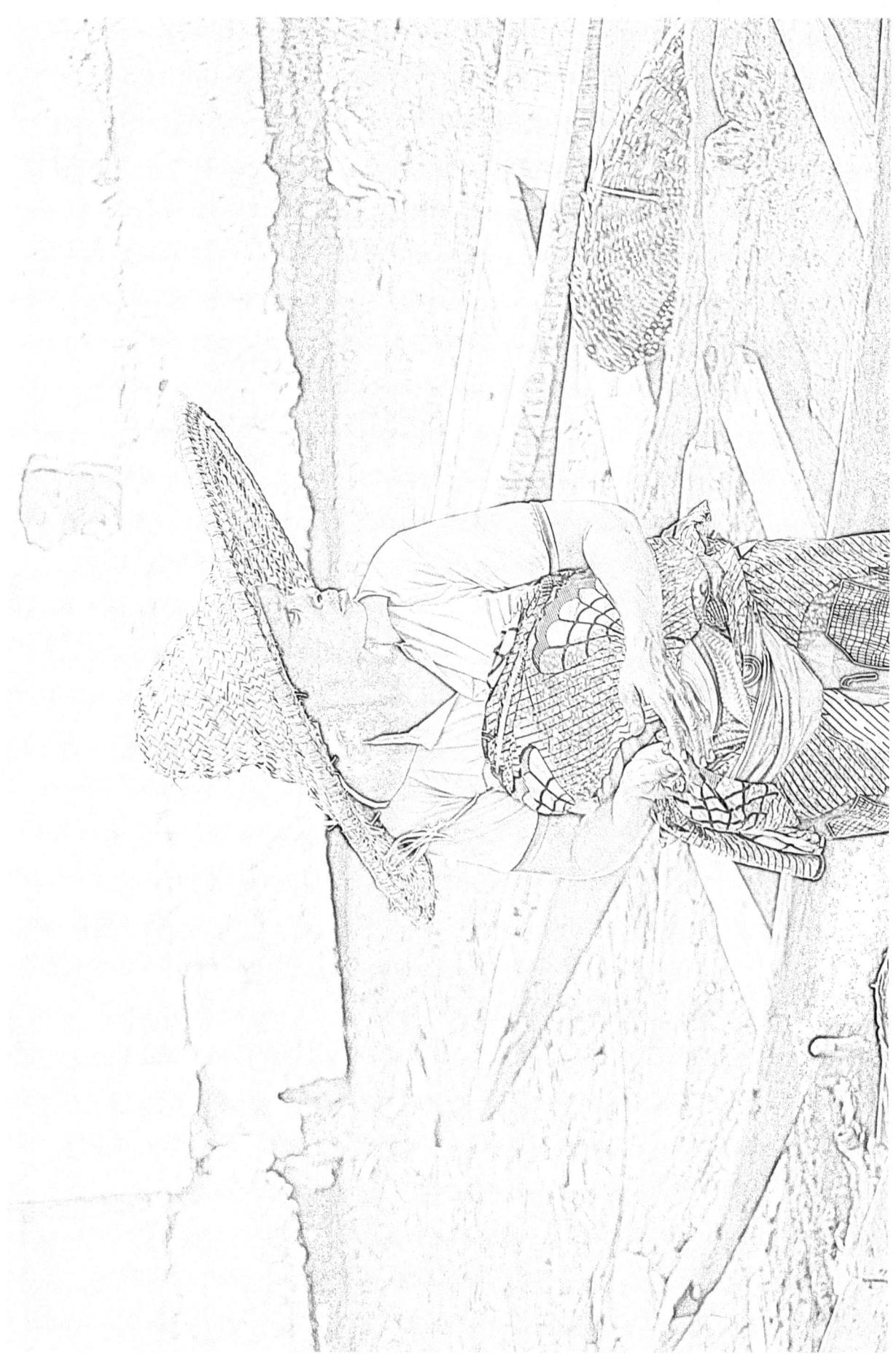

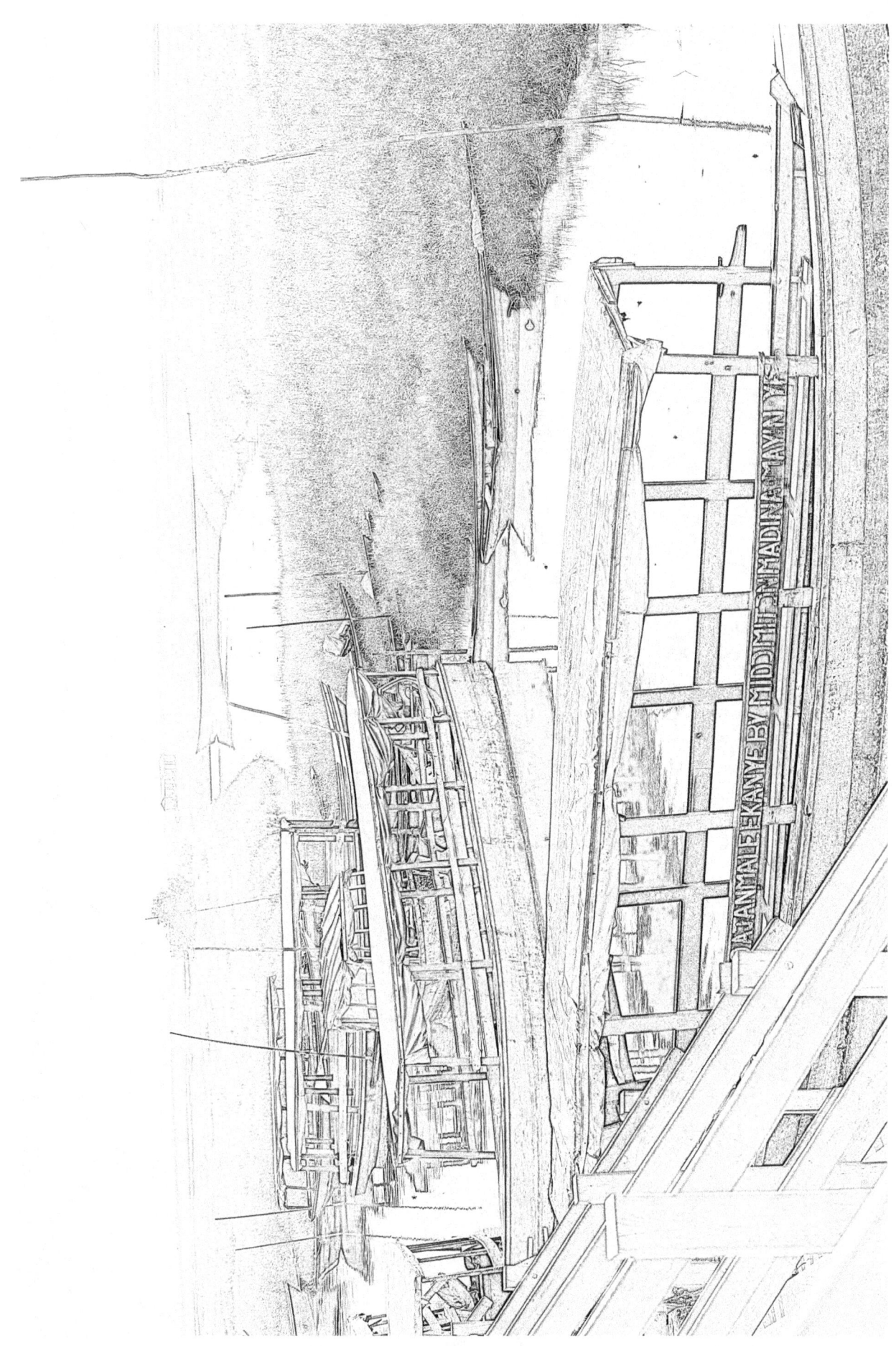

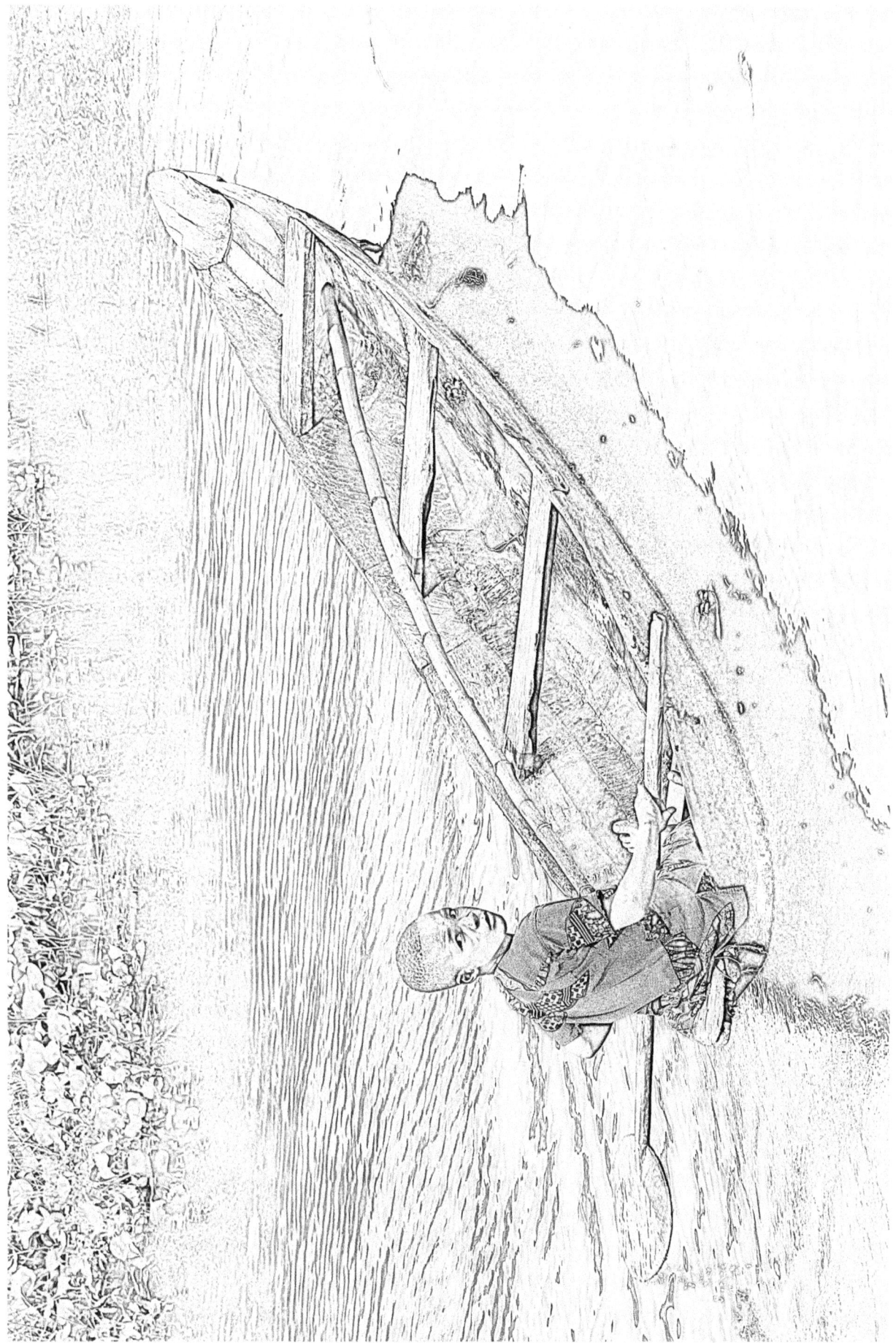

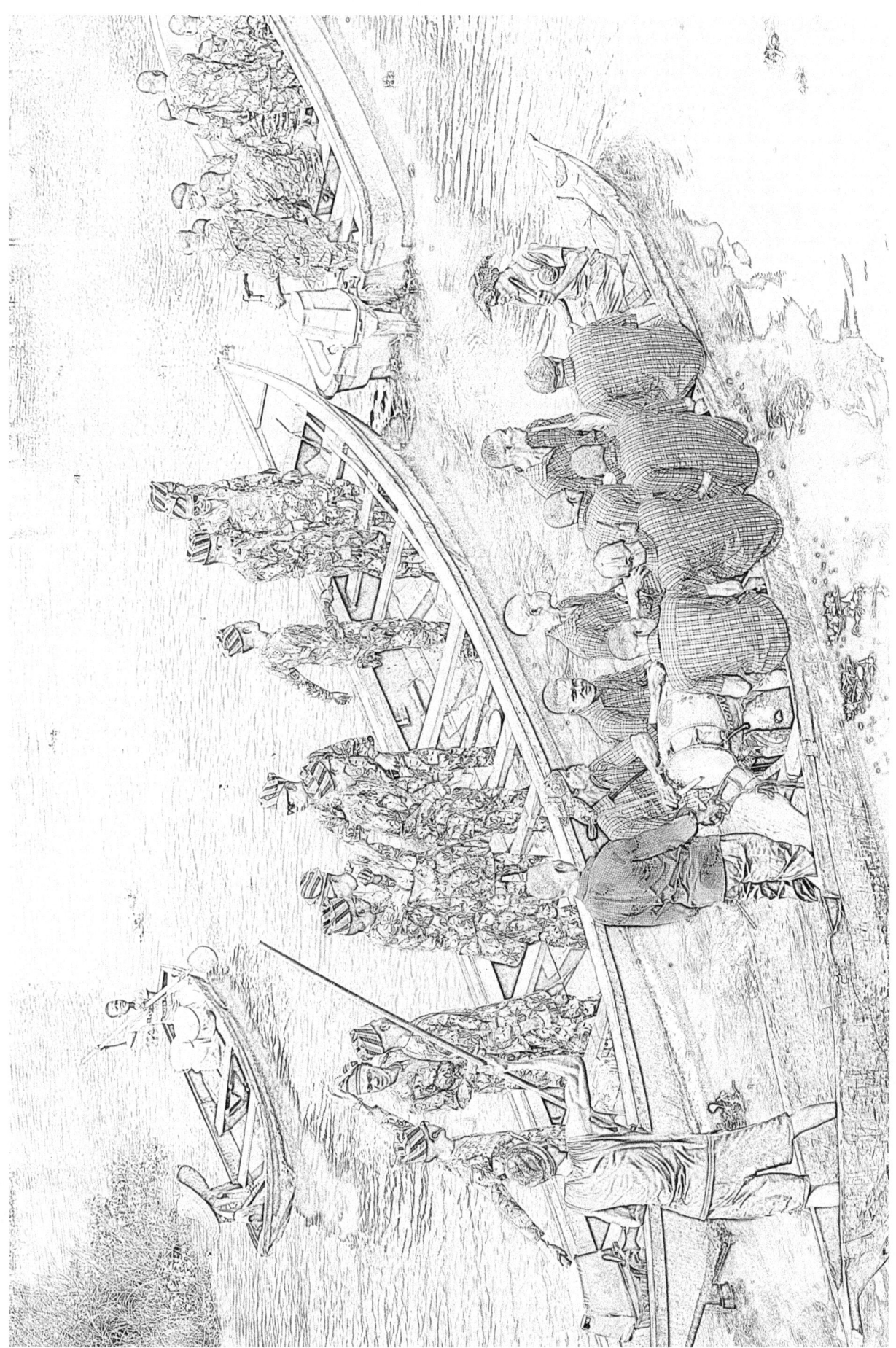

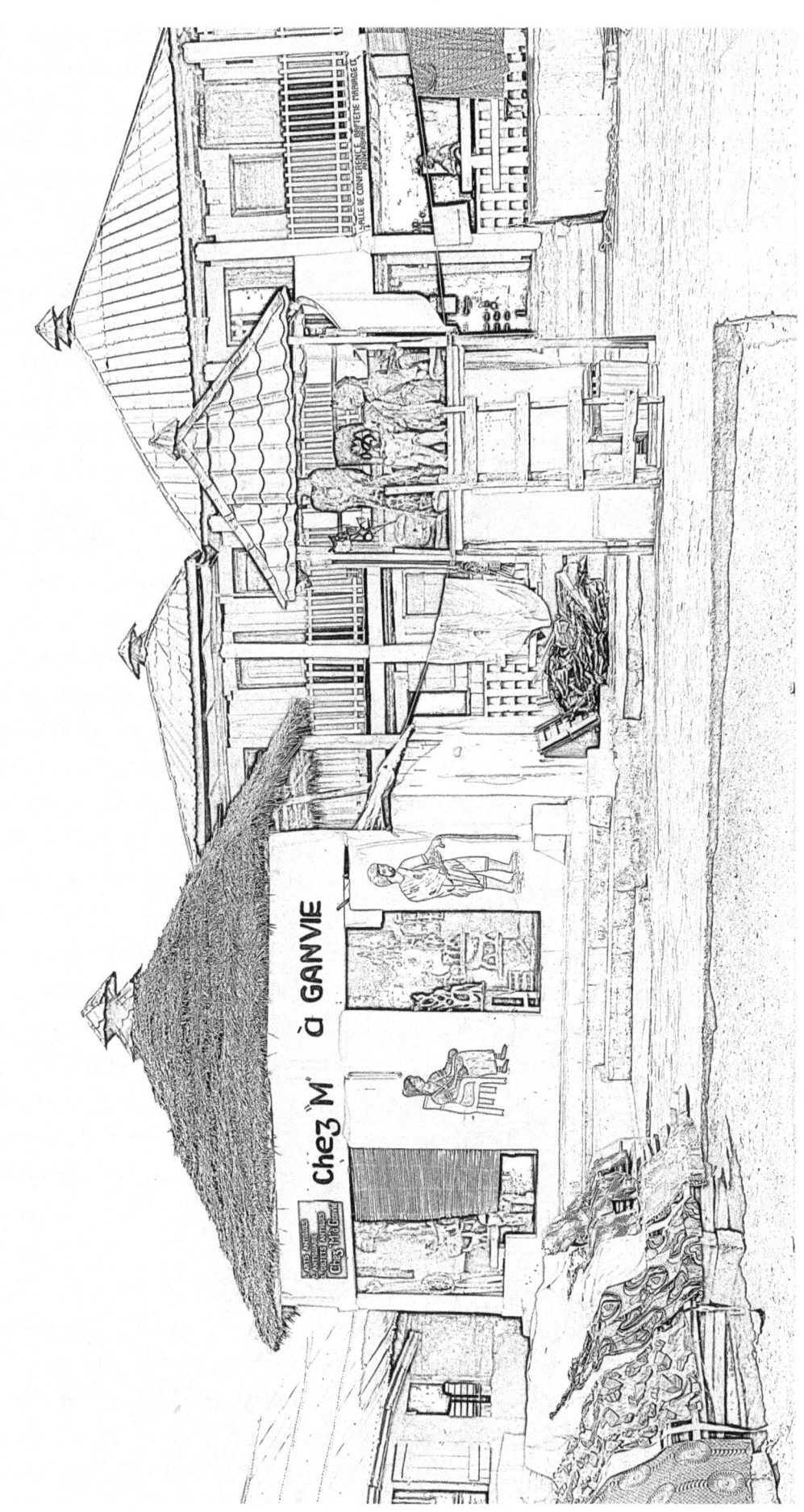

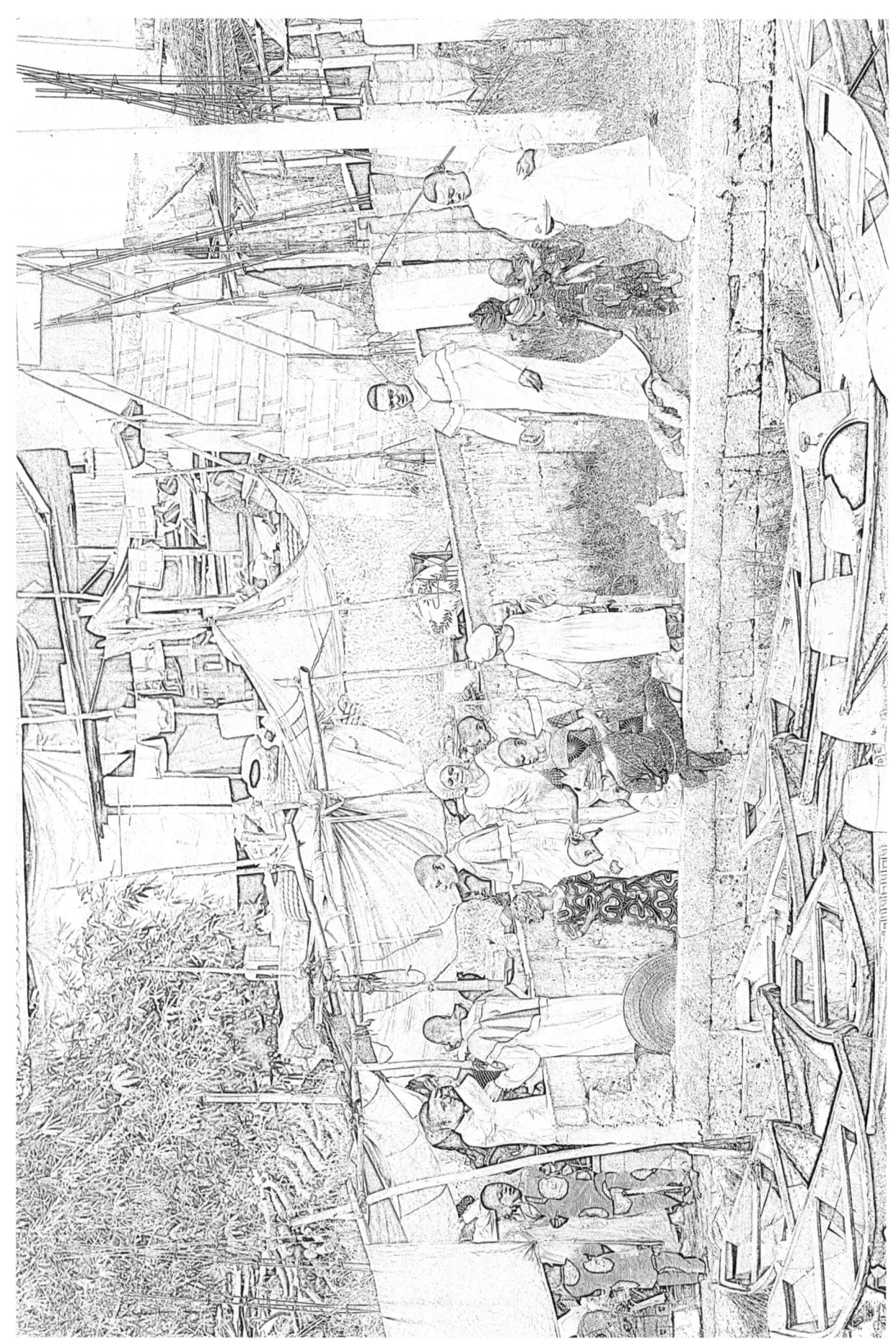